PARTON FAMILY HISTORY
England to Tennessee

By

Katherine Fletcher

INTRODUCTION

This follows the Parton family direct line from their arrival in 1609 in Jamestown, Virginia to the Great Smokey Mountains of East Tennessee. They survived the Jamestown Indian Massacre in 1620 and lived productive lives. Follow with me through eleven generations of Parton's and discover their lives and contributions to American history. This family lived in Sevier County, Tennessee for many generations and also includes the family of Dolly Parton, the famous singer and songwriter.

HISTORY OF THE PARTON FAMILY

The Parton family name originates from England as far back as the 11th century. The Norman name Partant is the origin. They held a family seat in Cumberland, England near Whitehaven and were Lords of the Manor of Parton.

NOTE TO READERS

Please keep in mind that not all public records are accurate. There are often mistakes in name spellings and dates of birth and death. Even from one census record to the other the information changes. Genealogy is never 100 percent accurate. However I have followed the documented records of this line and believe this to be mostly accurate.

PARTON FAMILY GENEALOGY

GENERATION ONE: George Melvyn Parton and Hattie Roberts

GENERATION TWO: Joseph Estes Parton and Elizabeth Betsy Jenkins Fronaberger

GENERATION THREE: William H. Parton and Nancy Elizabeth Paine

GENERATION FOUR: Moses Parton and Mary J. Horsley

GENERATION FIVE: John Parton

GENERATION SIX: John Benjamin Partain and Alice K. Stanley

GENERATION SEVEN: Robert Partain IV and Cindy Kelsey

GENERATION EIGHT: Robert Partin III and Elizabeth Rawlings

GENERATION NINE: Robert Partin II Mary Alice Reviea

GENERATION TEN: Robert Partin Sr. and Margaret Hayle

GENERATION ELEVEN: Robert Partin 1560-1617 born in England, arrived in VA in 1609 in Jamestown

GENERATION TWELVE: John Parton

BELOW ARE THREE FAMILY TREE CHARTS COVERING ELEVEN GENERATIONS.

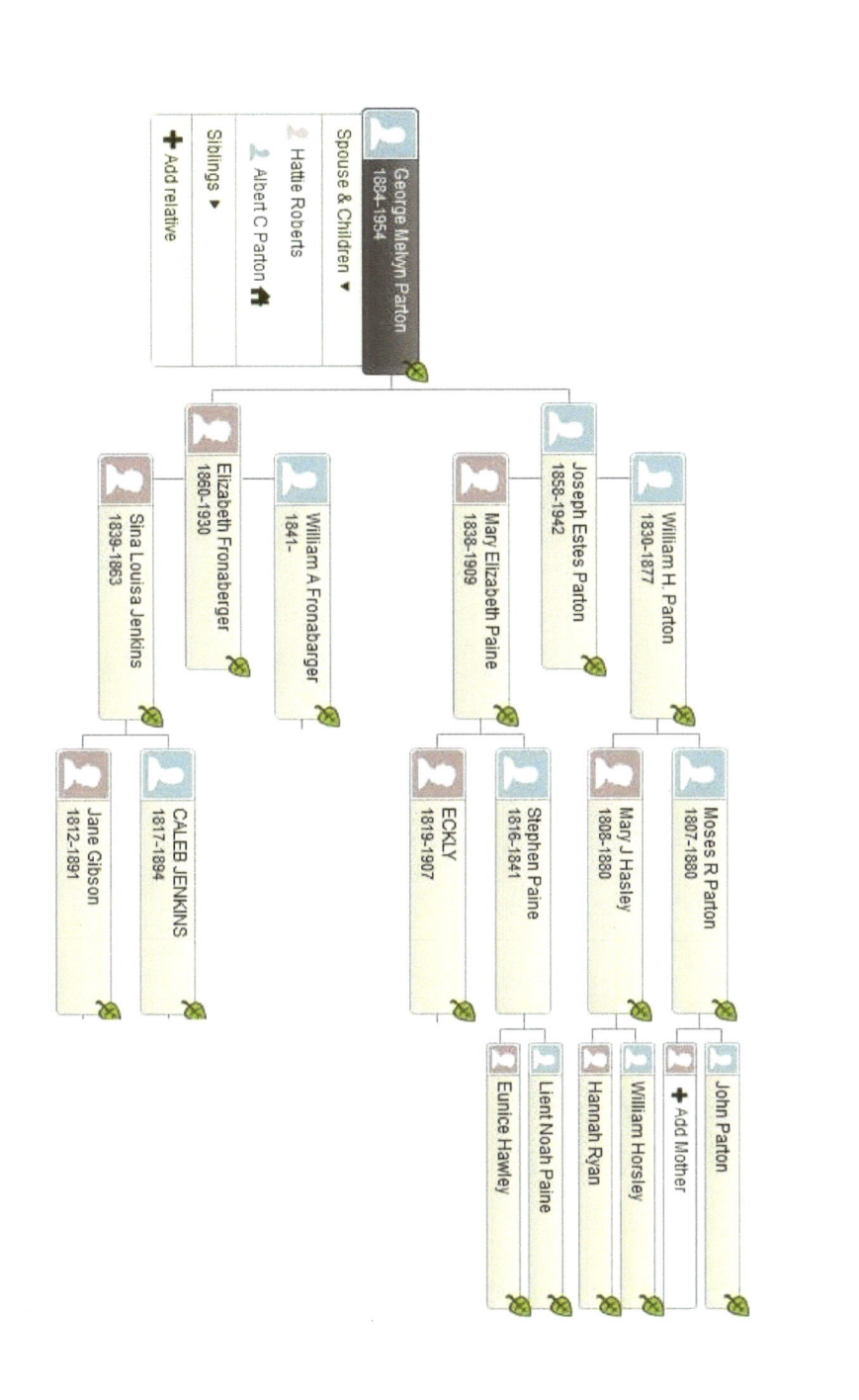

George Melvyn Parton
1884-1954

Spouse & Children ▼
Hattie Roberts
Albert C Parton
Siblings ▼
Add relative

Elizabeth Fronaberger
1860-1930

William A Fronabarger
1841-

Joseph Estes Parton
1858-1942

Mary Elizabeth Paine
1838-1909

William H. Parton
1830-1877

Sina Louisa Jenkins
1839-1863

Jane Gibson
1812-1891

CALEB JENKINS
1817-1894

ECKLY
1819-1907

Stephen Paine
1816-1841

Mary J Hasley
1808-1880

Moses R Parton
1807-1880

Eunice Hawley

Lient Noah Paine

Hannah Ryan

William Horsley

Add Mother

John Parton

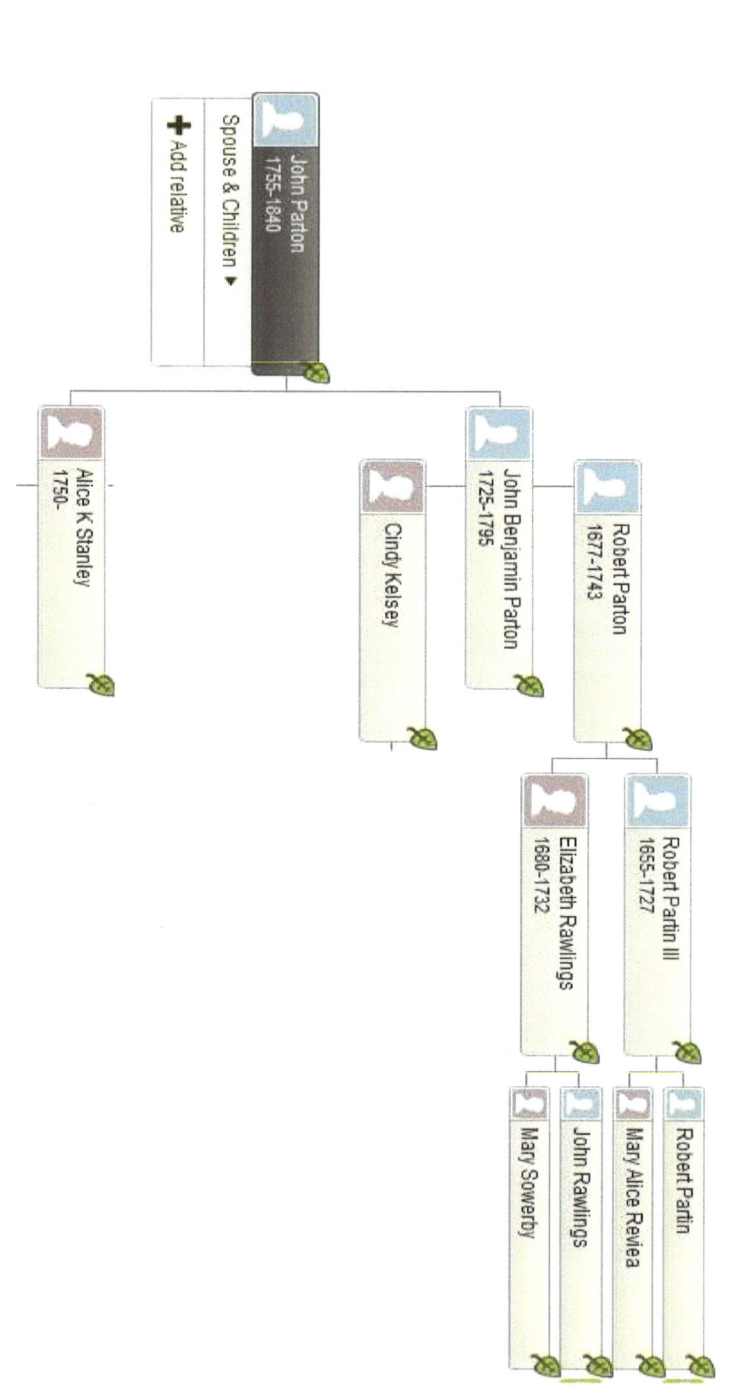

John Partin
1540–

Robert Partin
1560–1617

Spouse & Children ▼

(Unknown parent)

👤 Robert Partin

➕ Add relative

GENERATION ONE

George Melvyn (Melvin) Parton (10/4/1884) Sevierville, TN to 1/3/1954 Sevier Co, TN and Hattie Roberts (1884-1952).

George married Mary Ann Bentley and had four children.

His second wife is **Hattie Roberts** born 1884 in Tennessee. Hattie Robert's parents are Lloyd Roberts and Mary Reed. The Robert's are connected with the Atchley family. Hattie died in 1952 at 71 of a brain hemorrhage and hypertension.

Children with Mary Ann Bentley:

Robert 1896-
Mary Ann 1897-
Berta 1900-
Lucy 1912-

Children with Hattie Roberts

Bill Parton
Chris
Ernest
Gladys – 1919-1982 / married Edward M. Glandon

Jane – 1910-1960 / married Culla Huskey (this could be Horsely)

Lola – married David Morris "Joe" McMahan

Albert Crisperdell 1908-1948 / married Marie Gunnels. Marie Gunnells family was part Cherokee, Mohawk and Iriquois.

GENERATION TWO

Joseph Estes Parton (4/15/1858) Sevier Co, TN and died June 1942 in Jefferson County, TN (Dandridge). His wife was Elizabeth Betsy Jane Jenkins Fronaberger (1860-1930).

Their Children:

Mary Elizabeth
Willie Russell 1878-1937 married Laura Rebecca Kirby
Louie Ellen 1882-1908
George Melvyn 1884-1954
Dossie Alice 1886-1968
Joseph Estes 1888-1960 died in Kentucky

GENERATION THREE

William H. Parton (1/15/1830) born Burke County, NC and died 5/9/1877 Sevier County, Tennessee.
Wife Nancy or Mary Elizabeth Paine (12/28/1838) in Indiana and died in 1/13/1909 in Tennessee.

Their children:

Joseph Estes Parton 1857-1942 Sevier Co, TN married Betsy Jenkins.

Rev. George L. Parton 1858-1950 Sevier Co, TN to Jefferson Co, TN

William Brazelton Parton 1860-1927 Sevier Co, TN

Frances C. Parton - 1865-1937 Sevier Co, TN

Mary Elizabeth - 1866- Sevier, Co, TN

Andrew E. - 1870 Sevier Co, TN

Martha Ellen 1873-

Erastus Brownlow Murphy 1881

David Monroe - 1871-1959 Sevier Co, TN married Sarah Etta Keasling. Here's his family picture.

FAMILY PICTURE OF DAVID MONROE PARTON

The grave of William Parton.

GENERATION FOUR

Moses Parton (4/22/1806) born in Burke County North Carolina and married 1828 and died 1880 in Tennessee. In the 1830 census he was in NC, 1840 census was in York, SC working in a technical trade. 1850 census was Greene County, TN and 1860 he lived in Sevier Co. Tennessee.

This branch of the Parton family is known as the Sugarland's group.

First Wife: Nancy Clabough

His wife Mary J. Horsley born 1808 North Carolina and died 1880 Sevier Co, TN. She is perhaps the daughter or relation to Hannah Ryan Hostley, late wife of Rev. War Soldier Birch/Burch Allison. Mary Horsley was the sister to his brother John Cook Parton.

Also has wives listed as Mary A. Barton 1830, Mary Horsley 1828, Mary Cole 1841.
unsure if this is true

Their children:

John Benjamin Parton 1829-1907

Andrew W. -1831-1877

Nancy M. 1832-1913

Benjamin F. 1834

David M. 1835-

Albert Huston Parton 1837-1910 –there is a story that he joined the Civil War (Union) and disappeared for many years after the war. He did not want to return to his wife, Sarah Evans Parton and let her believe he was dead. She lived in Emerts Cove, Sevier Co. His family told her that he was dead. He apparently lived for a time at his Uncle Wash Crum's near the Nolichucky River. The Parton's lived on both sides of the Nolichucky River in Greene Co, TN.

Rachel P. Parton 1838-1839

James E. 1839-1940

Alexander R. 1841-

Mary L. 1850-1905

GENERATION FIVE

John Parton 1754/62-1846 born in Southwarke Parish, Surry County, Virginia and lived in Cocke County and Greene County, TN. He died in Greene, Murray Georgia. Census records show John living alone and widowed age 91 in Union Point, Georgia in 1840. Union Point was originally called Scruggsville.

I don't know who his first wife was. His second wife, but not the mother of these children was Talitha Price. Records from Georgia indicate Talitha died in 1839.

John fought in the War of 1812.

Wife #2 is Talitha Price born 1786 Richland County, SC. marriage date 3-31-1807.

His children:

George Gabriel - 1790 Burke Co., NC married Ann Lough (Portuguese). Cocke Co, TN and Pope Co, AR. His descendants use the name Partain.

James Paton 1790/1800 Burke Co, NC married Isabella Edmiston/Edmundson. In Burke Co, NC in 1840 and 1850 has them in Greene Co, TN and Walker County, Georgia at Lafayette. Descendants are from Cocke Co, TN and Walker Co, GA.

Benjamin Parton 1801 North Carolina / died Sevier Co, TN married Hannah Cole. This is singer Dolly Parton's line. In fact Benjamin and Hannah are Dolly Parton's third times great grandparents. Their son, Benjamin continues the Dolly Parton line and was a survivor of the Civil War after being shot in the head. Benjamin witnessed Moses's marriage in Burke Co, NC in 1828. In 1830 he was in Cocke Co, TN and in 1840 Greene Co, TN. Descendants use Parton spelling. Benjamin's son Elisha was a prisoner of war for two years in Andersonville, Georgia. Elisha was married to Martha Whaley. He did not survive the worst civil war prison in the country, Andersonville, Georgia. He died in 1864. This family is part of the Sugarland group of Sevier County, TN. There is a record that shows Benjamin was a migrant farm worker.

Moses R. – 10-22-1807 Burke Co., NC died 1880 in Sevier Co, TN (aged 72) married Mary Hasley - also related to the Allison/Ellison line.

THE PARTON CEMETERY IN GREENBRIER

John Cook Parton – 1808 Burke Co., died 1885 Nodaway County, Missouri. John married Anna (Hanna) Ellison/Allison, daughter of Revolutionary War Soldier Birch/Burch Allison and Hannah Ryan Hostley. John was in Burke Co, NC in 1830 near brother Randall.

Serena – 1814 North Carolina married John Hicks/Hix and lived in Cocke Co, TN. Had a son George Gabriel Hicks.

Randall Emanuel- 1814 in NC married Nancy Goodson. Her parents were Matthew Goodson and Celia. Randall was born in Burke County, NC and migrated to Tennessee. Two of his sons fought in the Civil War. After Randall and wife died their children are raised by the Goodsons.

Elizabeth

Eli – 1819 - married Mary Ann Borden McCoy in Greene Co, TN. Died in Hamilton Co, TN.

Candace – 1821 in TN / married George Washington Crumb/Crum in Greene Co, TN. Her nephew, Albert Huston Parton lived with her and her husband while letting his wife think he was dead.

William born in NC, in 1822 Greene Co or Cocke County, TN married Sarah Baker who was related to the Evans and Love family. Sarah and William belonged to a church at Wittenburg in Greene Co, TN.

GENEATION SIX

John Benjamin Partain (1725-1830) and Alice K. Stanley (1750).

John was born in Surry, Virginia and died in Halifax, North Carolina.

Their children:

John Parton (1755-1840)

GENERATION SEVEN

Robert Partain IV (1680-1743) and Cindy Kelsey – born in Surry, Virginia, dead in Surry, VA.

Apparently he was also married to a second wife Jennifer Reed Grogan.

Their children:

William Cocke Partin
Robert
Lucy
Charles
Elizabeth Wyatt
John
Robert

GENERATION EIGHT

Robert Partin III (1655-1727) and Elizabeth Rawlings (1680-1732) born in Surry, VA and died in Sussex Virginia.

Elizabeth Rawlings 1705 - Surry County, Virginia
Father: John Rawlings Mother: Mary Collier
Born: 1680 - Surry County, Virginia
Died: 1733 - Surry County, Virginia
The Rawlings family originally comes from London and Lancashire England.

GENERATION NINE

Robert Partin II 1623 in Sherley Hundred VA died 1687
Surry, VA.   Arrived in Virginia in 1648. and Mary Alice
Reviea 1623 Charles City, VA and died 1687 Surry, Va.

Children:

Thomas Partain 1646-1646
William Partain 1648-1648
Mary Partain
Francis
Samuel
Charles
Robert (1655-1727)
John (1659-

GENEATION TEN

Robert Partin Sr. (1588-1650) and Margaret Hayle (1592-
1648)
Born in Bristol, Somerset, England and died in Isle of
Wright, Surry, VA.

Robert Partin came to America on the ship "Blessinge". He
was 21 years old and came from London, England.   In
1609 he arrived in Jamestown Virginia and was an
indentured servant. Robert was one of 80 people who
survived out of 400 people. At the end of his indenture
(usually 3 years) he got 100 acres of land in Charles City,
Virginia. His wife Margaret came to Virginia in 1617 and
they got another 50 acres. One of Robert's servants was
Thomas Hayle.

According to the 1624 records Robert and his family owned a house in West Shirley Hundred, Charles City, Virginia. The records also reveal he had 20 pounds of lead and two pounds of powder, a Snaphance firearm and several pieces of armor. He also has 3 cows, chickens and one pig.

Robert Partin, Sr.
Born: 1587 About 35 miles north of Bristol, England
Died: 1650 in Surry County, Virginia
Arrived in Jamestown on the Blessinge in 1609

Margaret Hayle 1619 in Sherley Hundred, Virginia
Born: 1588
Arrived in Jamestown on the George in 1617

The Hayle family comes from Northhamptonshire, England.

The Muster of 1624/5

Their children:

Avis 1619-1648
Rebecca 1619-1648
Robert
Deborah
Edward
Mary Webb
May
Ralph
Samuel
Robert

GENERATION ELEVEN

John Parton (1540-)   England and unknown wife.

FAMILY NOTES

FAMILY NOTES

OTHER GENEALOGY BOOKS BY KATHERINE FLETCHER

These books may be purchased at Amazon as a hard copy or Kindle download.

Rice Family History: Ireland to Virginia, NC and Tennessee

Turnage Family History: England to VA, NC, SC, TN

McCroskey Family History: Scotland to Tennessee

The Forbes Family History: Scotland to Tennessee

England, McKinney and Little Family History

The Lipp Family History: Germany to America

Perkins Family History: European Royalty to America

Kolmer Family HIstory Germany to America

Proctor Family History: England to Tennessee

Meade Family History: England to Connecticut

The Billingsley Family History: England to America

Trent Family History: England to Virginia to East Tennessee

IF YOU WOULD LIKE YOUR OWN FAMILY GENEALOGY DONE PLEASE CONTACT KATHERINE FLETCHER AT MISCKATE@GMAIL.COM.